FROM AN OYSTER TO A PEARL

AN INSPIRATIONAL STORY

VERONICA I. DIXON

From An Oyster to A Pearl: An Inspirational Story
Copyright© November 2013 Veronica Dixon

Published in the United States of America by
Gospel 4 U Publishing
www.gospel4unetwork.com

Gospel 4 U Network
www.gospel4uministry.com

Editor ~ Stephanie Montgomery (UC Concepts)
Photos Taken by Walter Sansbury

Scriptures are taken from the
King James Version unless otherwise marked.
ISBN 978-0-9896249-8-5
Printed in United States of America
November 2013

**For Bookings and engagements please
contact: fromanoystertoapearl@gmail.com**

CONTENTS

FOREWORD

The title of this book tells a lot about the author; Veronica Dixon is a breath of fresh air to everyone that knows her. She is a strong-willed and ambitious woman that I can truly call my friend. I was blessed to have met her about two years ago. She is a wife, mother, sister, cousin and friend. Veronica has a compelling story to tell in *From an Oyster to a Pearl*, a story that many would choose to keep to themselves after such a long period of silence. I believe by telling her story she can and will inspire other young women to speak out about tragic events that have taken place in many of our lives.

Sometimes as women and adults we bury our hurts and pain with the thought of not ever speaking about the details, thinking that they will go away without being addressed. *From an Oyster to a Pearl* touches on experiences and emotions that many of us have dealt with but refuse to tell anyone for fear that we will be blamed.

Pass the word around about this book and don't be afraid to make this a roundtable conversation with your young children, family, friends, students etc. I think we can all say we know someone this book relates to, so if you find as much as a sprinkle of you or anyone you know in these pages, don't be afraid to talk to someone about it.

Ms. Michelle Middleton
Customer Service Representative

Acknowledgments

This book would not have been written without the individual pearls God brought into my life, the ones who modeled love for me as a way of life. The first acknowledgment is to my Heavenly Father, for giving me the opportunity and vision to write "From an Oyster to a Pearl". Without Him, none of this would be possible.

I would like to thank my husband, Fontaine Earl Dixon, for his love through this journey, his encouraging words and his listening ear. I love you honey and I thank God for you every day! I would also like to thank my daughter, Leana R. Sullivan; she is my princess and my reason for smiling. Leana, this book is especially for you. Thank you for believing in me, and I pray that one day you will be the pearl God intended. Mommy loves you, and anything is possible through Christ Jesus.

Enormous thanks to my parents for believing in me and pushing me to finish the race. To my mom, Sara Lopez and Mrs. Holly Mangigan, thank you for being the loving pearls in my life. I thank God for you daily. I thank you for your sacrifices and strength that guided me through my journey. To my fathers; Sergio Gonzalez, Carlos Lopez and Pastor Leon Mangigan, thank you for your love and encouragement.

To my personal pearls: Sergio Gonzalez Jr., Monica Hargrove, Mrs. Yvette Jones, Walter Sansbury, Rosie and Ewe. I am humbly thankful for all the thoughts, prayers, belief and words of encouragement. Without you, "From an Oyster to a Pearl" would have never been shared.

Special Thank You

A special thanks to all the readers. I want to personally thank you for taking the time to read "From an Oyster to a Pearl." I would like you to know that while I was writing this book, God had you in mind. We never understand His will, but when we see the end result, that is when we are able to say Thank You - but my prayer is that you have learned how to say thank you through your pressures, and pain of life. Thank you for taking the time to read and I pray that my testimony is able to impact you, because then my pain was worth going through. Love always yours truly, Veronica

(Pearl of great value)

My Life's Scripture

Jeremiah 29:11 " For I know the plans I have for you, " declares the Lord, "plans to prosper you and not to harm you, plans to give you hope and a future."

Chapter 1

The History of the Pearl and My Life

$\mathcal{A}$s you enter into my history, I would like to share how my past parallels with the history of the pearl. I pray that you will see yourself through this path as well. Oysters are not the only type of mollusk that can produce pearls. Clams and mussels can also produce them, but it is a rare occurrence. Most pearls are produced by oysters in both fresh and saltwater environments. As an oyster's internal anatomy grows, so does its shell. The mantle is an organ that produces the oyster's shell by using minerals from its food. The material created by the mantle lines this shell. The formation of a natural pearl begins when a foreign substance slips into the oyster between the mantle and the shell and irritates the mantle. The oyster's reaction is to cover up the irritation to protect itself. The mantle then covers the irritation with layers of the same nacre substance that was used to make the shell. This continues until a pearl is created. Without this irritation penetrating the shell, the pearl would not exist. When the oyster reaches two to three years old, it can start its occupation of pearl growing. Water temperature is very important. Oysters need warm water while creating the pearl. About seventy-five degrees is ideal and sudden temperature changes can affect the quality of the pearl or even kill the oyster. It takes layer upon layer of nacre for a pearl to be created. If the oyster is disturbed, inspected or opened too quickly, the pearl will not be complete.

You might ask yourself what does a pearl have to do with me, a twenty-eight year old woman born in Newark, New Jersey? The history of the pearl is very similar to mine and a wonderful representation of God's plan in my life. One thing that comes to mind when I think of the history of the pearl, is how the oyster must experience the discomfort to produce the beautiful orb. My hard shell was developed from rejection, pain, manipulation and even deceit. Something had to penetrate that hard shell for it to create something of value and beauty. That pain and pressure was the beginning of the pearl. I invite you into my sea and peer through the shell and see the wonderment of God's amazing hand in my life's journey.

Now I want you to travel with me into my history. I was born at Newark Hospital in Newark, New Jersey. My mother, Sara, gave birth to a healthy little girl. I was her second child and only daughter. My parents welcomed my birth and the growth of their little family.

This was my first learned experience of a family. In the beginning, my mother worked two jobs and we hardly saw her except on the weekends. As would be expected, I gravitated to my father and my father naturally fell into being my primary caregiver. Early on, I remember being extremely close to my father. As it was told to me, I was a very bold little girl - not afraid of much, always showing off for my dad and seeking his approval. I enjoyed all the time spent with my father. I had a pretty simple life, or so it seemed. Like a minute speck of sand silently penetrating the oyster's mantle and settling into the shell to initiate the pearl, my life began its journey of the same arduous path.

Before too long problems arose that began isolating me from my family and friends. I started having difficulties processing information. My speech became almost intelligible and only my parents were capable of understanding me. School became a daily burden and an almost impossibility. I can remember feeling left out and disconnected with the other children. My inability to verbally communicate caused my extended family to shun me and even refuse the childcare my parents depended upon. I can remember being very young and my father sneaking me into his work because he was the only one who would watch me. Even though I was not able to comprehend what was going on, I was able to notice that something was missing. I thought perhaps it was taken from me, removed because I had been naughty or simply not good enough like everyone else. Because of my issue with communication I started feeling like I had to fight for attention. My father could sense my frustration and always made sure that he showed me acceptance and love. He knew I needed an outlet to convey my feelings and emotions. His plan was to have me explore my feelings through dance. The freedom in dancing is what I enjoyed most. It really helped me to feel wanted and accepted. It became my secret passion as I got older. To this day, I am happiest when I can express myself through movement and music.

As you see, this pearl began with rejection. Rejection through family and community is intensely devastating. This need for attention and feelings of being wanted would come to have a huge impact throughout my life. I call this layer of pain and exclusion, the sea of death. Your growth and change depends on how long you are allowed to develop before you leave the sanctuary and safety that surrounds you. Please understand if you are in this stage - endure, because you too are being created into a beautiful pearl.

AUTHOR VERONICA DIXON

Chapter 2

Who is the Oyster?

*F*irst, let me say that oysters live in the sea within a shell attached to rocks and coral reefs. They have the ability to survive and adapt to poor water conditions, and the shell helps them survive outside the water. If an oyster is washed ashore during a low tide, the shell remains closed and the internal fluids remain intact and clean. This enclosed liquid provides oxygen and nourishment. The shell is the oyster's protection and home. Just like the oyster, I too created a shell used to protect me from the pain and abuse inflicted by others. My shell became my refuge and home. When I was nine, my family was dealt a devastating life-altering blow. My beloved father was convicted of a crime and would be sent to prison for the next eighteen years. The little bit of happiness and security I had was ripped from me, and I felt awash in a stormy sea of loneliness. As the months went by, the waves were strong and relentless. It soon became a reality that my father would be gone for a very long time and that affected me in so many negative ways. The one thing that I could count on – the one thing that was the most special and important to me, my only place of love and acceptance, was within my family. In my young mind I knew, no matter what I might have to go through, I would get the family I desired. This set off a series of events that would take me from one family to another searching for a replacement for what I once had.

My mother was now alone and the sole support for her children. Not knowing where to begin she reached out into her community and started attending church. Where she found solace, love and a new direction for her life - I found nothing. I was just going through the motions of life and doing what was needed so that no one would detect how I was hurting. Since my mother was doing it alone, I got a summer job to help purchase the things I would need for the following school year. I went to work for a family that owned a store downstairs from their home. For me, it felt like it was a home away from home, and I was part of the family. This became my second example of a family.

I can remember that fateful summer day… as if it were yesterday. I was cleaning and folding some clothes in the store, and the husband walked over and stood behind me. As

I turned to see what was needed, he quickly lowered his face and put his cold wet lips on mine. Everything stopped. Time no longer existed. My fear slammed into my chest and exploded outward like a million tiny stars. I felt my body tremble as I heard him repeat against my lips, "It's ok, it's ok, it will make you feel good and I know you need this." I begged him to stop. Please stop. He didn't. The time passed so woefully slow upon a sea filled with all the terror, horror and pain born from a soul being ripped from its place in humanity. It ended as many tragic stories of abuse do, the abused trying desperately to get away, the abuser admonishing them, "Don't tell anybody. They will all be mad at you. It's your fault."

I left as soon as I could get away. The frightened little girl inside me was broken, unable to be mended, lost in a sea of pain. So very scared, too frightened to talk because I did not want to cause more hurt to my family or any to his. My mind was numb; I was dead inside. My heart was broken, another family lost. I felt dirty. I was hurting physically and emotionally from what he had done. I remember going home to my room and I was alone and all I did was scream and cry until I fell into a fitful asleep.

Now you may ask yourself, "Why keep going back?" Well, when you are the victim of abuse and the warden of so many dirty secrets and lies, you fear discovery. If you act out of the ordinary you may become subject to scrutiny that would expose the truth. So it is easier to go and lie down and be abused than speak the truth and destroy more lives. Finally, one day I recall going to work with a definite precognition that it would be my last day there and I would be fired. I went to talk to him and just as I began speaking, his wife came in and questioned what we were talking about, and he replied, "Veronica was being fresh and I had to explain to her that she can no longer work for us." I will never forget how her face contorted as she reached out with an open palm and slapped me across my face. "Get out of my house," she spat, "You messed up my family." I went home and found that she called my mom and gave her side of the story. I never came out that day and told my mother about the abuse. For years I carried that burden. It wasn't until I was grown up that I was able to finally speak out about it.

In the meantime, I started acting out. I became very disrespectful and hard to manage. The words, "You messed up my family," haunted me for a long time. I would hear those words and it was like poison being shot through my body. I knew I was the victim, but during those moments I felt like I abused and mistreated a family. I started believing it was my fault. My shell became very hard and impenetrable. And yet - in all of that, I was in church Praise dancing and singing and doing things in the name of God, but I did not know God for myself. I was angry at Him for allowing these things to happen to me. My anger and self-hatred were wearing me down. I had several unsuccessful suicide attempts. I did not want to live. I was tired of the loneliness and feeling like failure.

My abuse did not stop. It just changed faces. I was now my own abuser. I could not deal with rejection. I would do or say anything not to be rejected. I went to school and felt rejected because of my lack of knowledge. I started to skip classes and stay home. I would do whatever it took to meet boys and solicit them for the attention I craved. I was always looking for my next quick fix. Only later would I come to the understanding that my addiction was a need for affection and attention by men. Any would do, but my preferences were for older men. I kept chasing the dream that I would find my father and finally have my family back.

During my father's incarceration he and I would exchange letters and occasionally get to visit. Those were the times I felt I could be myself, but it was when those doors shut and you have to leave - I could feel myself revert back to being a victim. Times were hard and my mother divorced my father. It saddened me, but at that point in my life I just wanted to see someone happy. I cried, but I knew this was something my mother had to do. You see a lot of people think that when a person goes to prison it is just them - but that is not true. When my father went to prison he took the whole family with him; my mother, brother and me. It was just that his prison was behind high walls and iron bars and mine was within myself. I felt I was on 'lock down' and I was not doing well.

My mother started moving on with her life. She started dating a man and I could see that she was happy. This made me fearful. I was worried that he would take my mother away like the police took my father. I was hard-hearted and mean and I wanted him out of my mother's life. I told him I did not like him, and I didn't want to give him a chance. Usually this would cause people to leave because they couldn't handle me, but he did not go - he stayed and stood his ground. In fact, he married my mother and became my stepfather. I had such mixed emotions about this. I could see the potential for a family, a father figure or even a friend. Unfortunately, by then, my mind and soul had been too abused and worn down to remember how to reach out and trust. I was angry inside; so very distorted, but I never let anyone see it. I was tired of people making promises and never keeping them. I felt like no one wanted me, and I felt all alone in my terror and in my pain. I was drowning in my sea of deceit.

My acting out and defiant behavior escalated. My mother, not knowing what to do for me, decided to send me to stay with a family friend in Alabama. He was a church pastor and had been the best man in my mother's wedding. He was nice - but again, because of my fear of men, it was very hard to trust. When my mother shared that that she was sending me away, my question was, "What could this man or his family do for me? What did this family know about me, why would they want to help me, who am I? I moved to Alabama and I met this man's family. Now mind you, where I came from was not pleasant. Looking in from the outside, my life seemed ok; but now I was entering into a home where they had a mother and a father (a good one at that) and they had children. This was the third example of a family I had in my life and it scared me.

I can recall starting a new school and feeling like a child when they go on the bus for the first time and they want their parents to be there, to comfort them and tell them it was going to be all right. I had no one. This family started showing me a different love. It was as if I could actually feel it. Warming me like rays from the sun shining on an upturned face. They were walking with me and talking with me, I felt for the first time in my life that I started living. I started going to church and even though I was so hurt, I knew that God was there and He was doing things to remind me how special I was. It was a feeling that no man could give me, young or old. I had to learn things over again. I put this family through a lot of pain, because I did not know how to accept love, or even what it looked like because love left me when I was nine. It was a constant struggle fighting with the old me, while the new emerging person wanted so desperately to fit in. It was hard being away from my mother. Sometimes I felt all alone on a deserted island. I didn't hear from her as much as I would have liked to. The only thing I had to grab on to was this family; I pushed through my fears and really tried to accept the fact that this was my life. My thoughts kept clouding over and I was surrounded by lies that I told myself. You are worthless. No one wants you. Yet, there was something about this home.

I continued to mistreat myself and my new family. I would sleep around and act like I was someone else and lie to be accepted. They didn't go anywhere. Every time I would mess up, they stood by me and continued to love and support me. I recall one night when my mom was scheduled to call and didn't. It was quite the blow to my psyche. It caused such a severe reaction that I instigated a fight at the house and promptly ran away. I was done. I didn't want to look back. It was easier for me to hurt myself than someone else. I walked to a local restaurant to get a drink and plan my disappearance. While sitting at the table, the pastor calmly walked in and sat down and we talked. I shall never forget that powerful conversation. He said "Veronica, you are special, God has such a powerful calling on your life and the devil would do anything to see you destroy yourself." He explained that he understood I felt lonely, hurt and bitter - but that he and his wife would be there for me through anything. I went home and I felt as if my life was given back to me; I was worthy of a second chance and I could begin to make the right choices. I'm not saying that life became blissful, but I had a different perspective and I had a different drive. This Pastor was a reflection of Christ's Love. He never judged me once. He always just saw what I was called to do, not what I was at that moment. So when he spoke to me, he spoke to the woman that I would be - not the young, struggling person before him. My respect for him and his wife was immeasurable. I would have done anything for them.

When my life started having value and things were looking up, my mother decided to move to Alabama. Like a normal teenager was away from their parents, I was excited to be reunited but also fearful. I now had my family - my 'new' family. I felt they had given birth to the 'new' me, and I did not want to return to the old. When they told me I was moving back with my mother, I did not think she would accept me. Here I am, a teenager going back to a home I had not been in for a couple of years; unsure of myself and now another adjustment. I couldn't cope and once more relapsed. I lost another piece of myself.

I was living with my mother in 2003. I was told that I could be in the graduation ceremony with my class but wouldn't receive my diploma. I had not passed my graduation exams. I walked with my class and smiled for the pictures, but I felt like a failure. Who am I to be walking with them when what was in my folder was fake - like me. There is nothing like starting the next phase of your life with a huge deficit. I was already so far behind in so many aspects, I felt like I would never catch up. I had no prospects for my future and nothing holding me back when my brother invited me to come to visit him in Pennsylvania. My mother gave her approval so off I went. It was refreshing to visit and everything was good. I felt welcomed and at home. My brother and I spent a lot of time getting together with family. My aunts, uncles and cousins were all excited to see me. I was received with open arms and found great enjoyment with my family. I met many new people and had a newfound sense of freedom. Perhaps life could be good.

I returned home and everything was back to normal - or so I thought. The following month my cycle never started. I did not get my period. I was panicked and called my best friend. I told her what happened and she came over with the pregnancy test. It came out positive. I can still hear her breathless voice and see her head shaking in disbelief, "What are you going to do?" There was no hesitation on my part and I proclaimed, "I am moving to PA." And that was that. Divine intervention perhaps, I was resolute and had the rest of my life planned out before anyone could say anything. I told my mother, she was so hurt. There was nothing else for me to do, so I left. I felt like I was still running, but I was used to it now.

I moved to Pennsylvania. On March 30th, 2004 my life changed. I was given another chance. To me the humbling birth of my daughter was a sign from God. The God I heard about and felt in my heart was giving me the chance to live my life right. Shortly after giving birth to my daughter, I became a single mother and it was as if God had allowed me to go through that so I would not have any excuses to depend on anyone but Him.

After becoming a mother myself, I feel that was the time when God opened my heart and began speaking to me about my relationship with my own mother. My mother and I had a strained relationship for many years. Being a single parent she worked many long hours away from us, but she was doing what she needed to do to take care of her family. Sadly, I did not understand that at the time. For so many lonely years thinking my mom left me or had sent me away, was extremely difficult for me. I believed the one parent that should have been consistent with me was falling in the same category as everyone else. In retrospect a lot of my pain came from her choices. When I was sent to Alabama, hundreds of questions ran through my mind. I was in disbelief that a mother would send her child away to a family she did not know. At that moment, I couldn't fathom how that would help change my behavior or help me grow.

I often blamed her for not explaining the circumstances that caused my father to go to prison. Over sixteen years, I believed she held the key to my healing and she never opened that door. As an adult, I understand my mother did not know in detail what happened with my father. Therefore, my mother did not have the key, and she couldn't give me something she didn't have. She was fighting as hard as I to survive in her own private prison. I didn't blame my mother for my father's incarceration. It was just her lack of presence that affected me. Growing up I didn't have my mother as a social example. Things often done by females in my culture were foreign to me. She never taught me how to keep a house, cook, clean or do the things daughters often share with their mothers. Once I had my daughter, the relationship between my mother and I got better. Unfortunately, it was still strained and arduous, as I had so many unanswered questions. Only years later, was I able to reconcile my feelings with my mother.

When I became a single parent, life - none too kindly, told me it was now time to grow up. I didn't dare slip because I had a precious daughter that I vowed not to hurt and would always protect. My daughter and I started going to a church in Harrisburg and I liked it. It was not what I was used to. It was small and quiet and I couldn't do much there, but I know God wanted me there just to listen and learn. I would've never known what God had in store for me had I not met three, incredibly beautiful women. One of them I call my peace. She was quiet and private, and she would bring so much peace and calm to a room. The second was funny and had a heart of gold. She could always bring a smile to my face. The third was very personable and honest, a friend that speaks her mind and is faithful and supportive in friendship.

These women came into my life and spoke to my soul. Most importantly, they showed me what true friendship looks and feels like. They kept me accountable and taught me how I should be treated. One grew to become more than anyone ever had; she became my best friend. She began to teach me some of the most important life lessons; how to use money, to cook, to pray, to love, how to stand up for myself and use my voice, how to forgive and most importantly of all - how to be in love with Christ. They all showed me how to be a Proverbs 31 woman. They live and breathe the scripture Titus 2:4-5, "That they may teach the young women to be sober, to love their husbands, to love their children, to be discreet, chaste, keepers at home, good, obedient to their own husbands, that the word of God be not blasphemed." They embraced me and they continue to be beloved women in my life.

Of the three, my best friend was my angel. She managed her life all alone. She was a single mother of five, with one child that was profoundly disabled, and she set a strong example of how to be a good mother. One thing she would tell me often, "In order to grow, you will have to forgive your mother." I could tell her anything and not feel judged. I knew what she was saying was, "Regardless how much you love me, there will be a time when you reconnect with your mother and you will have to forgive her." I knew it would come to that one day. I had to empty my soul and forgive my mother. Once I opened that door I could begin to heal with her and get to know her. It was then I asked her to forgive me for everything I had done, she too apologized for her inabilities. She confessed she was never taught to parent and so she was learning as she was going along. I understood my mother acted out of desperation to do what she had to in order to survive and care for her children.

I am a true believer that what you learn growing up is what your children will learn from you. I saw that cycle with my parents. My mother was determined to break that cycle although I didn't recognize it then and it has taken God many years to help me understand what she was trying to accomplish. I sometimes put myself in my mother's shoes with Leana, my daughter. I can't imagine having to go through so much and still see your child suffer. You want to rescue them, but you yourself need rescuing. My mom found her strength through Christ. I am thankful for the bond with my mom, and I wouldn't change anything about it. We have grown to become best friends and someone I want to be around more and more. This all lends itself to my value and beauty as a pearl.

Now you know how I can compare my life to a pearl. God helped me like an oyster to give birth to the pearl. My past was like the ugly, irritating sand speck to an oyster. The pain and abuse and rejection allowed me to slowly grow and evolve into the pearl I am today. There was a time when I would sit alone in my room and cut myself. I could not deal with the pain of losing my father and of being raped. I did not want to live and I wanted to take my life. I felt as if no one would want me, that I was junk. I couldn't even handle the pressure and expectation that I put on myself. I wouldn't allow myself to feel worthy of any praise from others. My life was so false and full of lies, I was dying inside. It was when my daughter was born that I knew that my life had to change. I could not continue to be in a place of fear, doubt, and low self-esteem. I had to do something with myself. I had to try something new and look outside of myself. Once I had that ability, then I started seeing myself grow and mature.

One step in my growth journey came in February 2011. After eighteen years, my father was released from prison. When he was released, I too had a triumph as my self-imposed prison walls came tumbling down. Through Christ, I knew my sentence was over and I could have freedom. I was so very nervous. In the span of a second I went from a twenty-seven year old married woman, to a trepidacious youth of nine. Will he accept me? What happens now? Will he be proud of me? Most importantly, I wondered does he still love me. From the steps - just as I saw my father leave me so many years ago, I was now walking up the steps to see him. Nobody watching, no gates closing behind, no bars - it was just me and him.

Initially, I thought I had forgiven him; I was still harboring some anger, but this time there was no turning back. I had to deal with it head on. The difference was I now had Christ to help me. I asked my dad to come to my house. I needed to speak to him in a place I felt safe and comforted. There, I would have my husband - supporting me, loving me, giving me strength. I now had to tell him how I was raped and the pain and frustration, my loneliness and years of trying to be someone that I wasn't. Amidst all this, my wonderful father looked at me and said, "Sorry", and "please forgive me". It felt like the flood gates opened and the sorrow began washing away. I know that I have been forgiven because I was able to make a leap of faith to completely and honestly forgive all that had happened. I know that my father loves me and now we are able to speak openly about our lives. One thing he taught me is how to not make excuses, but to really embrace life lessons. I am not perfect but I know that I have

the support of my parents and family and most important –
God, who allows me to conquer anything.

While my family was now returned to me, a piece was
still missing. It was my sister, who my father had from a
previous relationship. The Lord allowed me after twenty-one
years of separation, to find her in 2012. My last recollection
I had was that we were close, but years and things have
happened. I didn't want to reach out to her and overstep any
boundaries. I decided to pray and ask God for wisdom. While
praying I felt God was telling me I was prepared and ready
for this. This meant I was fully healed and I wouldn't be
reaching out in anger, and we both deserved this. I saw her
online and knew in my heart that she was my sister. I sent her
a message and she replied. I was so overcome with emotion,
all I could do was cry. It was as if we had picked up where
we left off. You could tell we were both nervous, but God
had brought us together for a reason and we were willing to
do anything to not lose each other again. It brought to my
mind the scripture John 10:10 which says, "The thief comes
not but to steal, to kill and to destroy, but I come that you
may have life and life more abundantly." I felt like God came
in and gave both of us life and love, and what the enemy was
meant to kill did not happen. God meant for us to meet so we
could give him the glory. I am amazed with what God has

done with the friendship between my sister and I. God has laid the foundation down and opened a door for us to begin praying and healing together. God can restore any relationship. He is the author and finisher of our faith and if we ask Him for wisdom, He will give it to us. There is nothing too hard for God. The pearls that we become are a testament to His healing love and grace.

AUTHOR VERONICA DIXON AND HER
BEAUTIFUL DAUGHTER
LEANA SULLIVAN

Chapter 3

Separating the Pearl from the Oyster

Once an oyster farmer decides it is time to harvest the pearls, the death of the oyster is inevitable. First it needs to be removed from its safe and secure environment in the sea. Death is just moments away as a sharp knife is slipped firmly between the two shells, breaking the seal and tearing them apart forever. As the unprotected oyster succumbs to death, a beautiful pearl can finally be released from its constraints. Just like the oyster died, I knew that I needed my past life shell of deceit broken away so I might emerge polished and blessed, saved by His grace.

For many years I heard the calling that was in my heart, but I became comfortable and I made myself believe I wasn't good enough for anything else. I would settle for the abuse and just learn to adjust. Isaiah 64: 8 says, "Yet you, Lord are our Father, We are the clay, you are the potter, we are all the work of Your hand." I had to realize that God was reshaping me and I started to see myself change. I know that God was creating a new heart for me. The Bible talks about this in Psalms 51:10, "Create in me a pure heart, O God and renew a steadfast spirit within me." Through Jeremiah 29:11 God told me, "For I know the plans I have for you, declares the Lord, plans to prosper you and not to harm you, plans to give you hope and a future." I knew that God was doing surgery on my soul. My spiritual father in Alabama preached from Philippians 3:13-14, "Brothers, I do not consider that I have made it my own, but one thing I do; forgetting what lies behind and straining forward to what lies ahead, I press on toward the goal for the prize of the upward call of God in Christ Jesus". I knew life would not be easy, but whatever God had planned for me was my goal. I had learned the lesson of the pearl. Through trials of great suffering and abuse, being beaten and broken by life and brought down by others, I could emerge anew. A priceless beauty brought forth through God's saving grace and everlasting love.

In 2006 I met a charming man. He came into my life and he showed me so much about life, respect and was a daily example of Christ's love. Two years later we stood in front of

God and our families and took our vows that we would hold on through better and for worse. I am so thankful my husband has stepped in and become the best step-father to Leana. He has wholeheartedly embraced the challenge of being the head of our home and the Godly-example that she needs to live her life for Christ. This is my fourth example of a family and it is mine.

One thing I know for sure is that nothing is too hard for God!

MY WONDERFUL FAMILY:
MYSELF, FONTAINE DIXON, &
LEANA SULLIVAN

Reflections

1. Who is your Oyster?

2. What pressures in your life are happening that are causing you to develop?

3. What did you learn "From an Oyster to A Pearl" that will help you develop your pearl?

4. What steps do you need to take to separate yourself from the Oyster, to be the Pearl God intended for you to be?

My prayer for you is that you are able to reflect back and see the things that you have been through or are going through and know that what is happening - is not meant to break you or hurt you, but it is meant to bring you value. My prayer is that you will be able to look at my life and all I have been through and really embrace what you are going through and that you will surrender yourself to Christ, because no matter what - the Journey will not be the same if He is not in it. From one pearl to another, know that you are valued and God has appointed this time in your life to develop you.

<u>Notes</u>

From An Oyster To A Pearl

_____

_____

_____

_____

_____

_____

_____

_____

_____

_____

_____

_____

_____

Prayer of Salvation

*D*ear God in heaven, I come to you in the name of Jesus. I acknowledge to you that I am a sinner, and I am sorry for my sins and the life that I have lived; I need your forgiveness.

I believe that your only begotten Son Jesus Christ shed His precious blood on the cross at Calvary and died for my sins, and I am now willing to turn from my sin.

You said in Your Holy Word, Romans 10:9, that if we confess the Lord our God and believe in our hearts that God raised Jesus from the dead, we shall be saved.

Right now I confess Jesus as the Lord of my soul. With my heart, I believe that God raised Jesus from the dead. This very moment I accept Jesus Christ as my own personal Savior and according to His Word, right now I am saved.

Thank you Jesus for your unlimited grace which has saved me from my sins. I thank you Jesus that your grace never leads to license, but rather it always leads to repentance.

Therefore Lord Jesus transform my life so that I may bring glory and honor to you alone and not to myself.

Thank you Jesus for dying for me and giving me eternal life. In your name I pray Amen.

You are a BEAUTIFUL PEARL In the making!

Veronica I. Dixon

www.ingramcontent.com/pod-product-compliance
Lightning Source LLC
Chambersburg PA
CBHW051712090426
42736CB00013B/2660